Job Lot of Rhymes

Cherry B

Illustrated by Fe Duncan

Flapjack Press
flapjackpress.co.uk

Exploring the synergy between performance and the page

Published in 2021 by Flapjack Press
Salford, Gtr Manchester
🌐 flapjackpress.co.uk
f Flapjack Press 🐦 FlapjackPress ▶ Flapjack Press

ISBN 978-1-8381185-4-9

All rights reserved
Copyright © Cherry B, 2021
🌐 cherrybpoet.co.uk
f cherryb 🐦 BCherry67 📷 mxcherryb

Illustrated by Fe Duncan
f damnedfineart 📷 feduncanillustrator

Photos & lyrics courtesy of the author

Cover image by Daniele Levis Pelusi
Courtesy of Unsplash
Manipulation by Brink

Printed by Imprint Digital
Exeter, Devon
🌐 digital.imprint.co.uk

This book is sold subject to the condition that is shall not by way of trade or otherwise be lent, re-sold, hired out or otherwise circulated in any form, binding or cover other than that in which it is published and without a similar condition including this condition being imposed on the subsequent purchaser.

A UNESCO City
of Literature

This book is dedicated to my dad Rodney,
who died suddenly in 2016.

His death made me try things I feared or avoided
and to acknowledge how precious time is.

To those who fear that they can't achieve their dreams
and goals – well, what is the worst that can happen
if you try or ask? If you don't, you will never know.
You *can* change your destiny, like in a 'choose your own
adventure book' – if you take the easy path and stay in
your comfort zone, you'll seldom learn about yourself.

I chose to live more instinctively and to see what could
possibly happen if I just asked.

Contents

About the Author	6
Introduction	7
Don't Make It Easy for Yourself	9
Early Days	**11**
Poetical Justice Fees	14
Innocence of Television	14
Lies Damn Lies	15
Sunny Delight	15
Spice Girls	16
Pregnant Pause	18
The Vegetarian	19
Barbara Cartland	20
MMM	22
Married Men	23
Let Us Pray	24
Bigots	25
Not in Our Back Yard	26
Justice Bill	27
True Blue	28
Cherry & Peesh	**29**
Punk Mum	30
PC World	33
Never Mind the Pistols	35
Cider for Breakfast	36
Poetry is the New Rock 'n' Roll	38
Yesterday's Kids	40
15	44
Ritchie Rehab	45
Trump Card	47

Society Anxiety	50
Loan Shark	52
Empty Windows	54
School Night Syndrome	56
Chemistry	58

Politics is Personal — **61**

Corbyn Crush	62
Let the Fascists In (?)	64
Terminus House	67
Starmer	70
Barbara Castle	72
The Tale of Yaxley Lennon	73
Who Voted Tory?	75
Wonderland is Calling	76

Poetry is Therapy — **78**

Charlie	80
Be Kinder	82
The F Word	84
The Family Group	86
You Don't Know How I Feel	89
SPAX	91
The Valley of Moral Damnation	92

About the Illustrator	*94*
A Friend Like Fe	*95*

About the Author

Bev Warner AKA Cherry B was born in Harlow, Essex. After failing to get into art college, she went to her hometown college and studied drama, photography and multi-media, and was elected secretary of their student union. It was while attending a conference in Blackpool that she met two girls from the North East, whom she then went to visit and stayed in the region for years, forging links maintained to this day.

After moving back to Harlow, Bev went through a challenging time in her life and her creativity began to rise. She even set up her own business called Funky Dunky, The Condom Co. – the first condomery in the UK. But she did not have a brain full of business plans, just random ideas, and eventually found her vocation in care work.

Bev went to university and graduated with more than just a BSc in Social Policy Research – her daughter Liberty. She began to take her poetic craft to stages around the country, often at comedy clubs and on punk line ups. During this time, Bev lost her son, who was stillborn, and although it gave her motivation to get out and achieve her goals, it also layered a deep vulnerability, which combined with a few bad gigs, a divorce and a full-time work and mother role, stopped her performing.

The next decade bought a new daughter, Ruby, and a career as Bev trained to be a psychotherapist and went back to uni to obtain her post-grad. Another decade on and she is performing poetry again, a part of genre-defying punk 'n' roll combo Cherry & Peesh, and a psychotherapist with her own private practice. Poetry spans Bev's personal and professional life; both are vital in wellbeing and reassurance.

Introduction

This book collates a mixed collaboration of poems and songs from the past three decades (albeit with a bit of a gap in the middle). From early awkward public readings, to being in a band. From when I began to brave the crowd and perform live, to performing at one of the largest punk festivals in the world.

After doing this for about five years though, I stopped performing for almost two decades: fear, self-doubt and lost confidence got to me after a dreaded 'bad gig' supporting Rich Hall in London; the crowd were definitely and defiantly not there to see a poet. I went away to have children and build a career, but my head was still full of rhymes and creative ideas…

It was the death of my dad in 2016 which made me realise that we have very few opportunities to fulfil our goals. I began to live my life in a different way and gave myself the freedom to rediscover my identity. I dyed my hair pink again, decorated my house in the style of an angry militant teenager and became never afraid to ask – because if I didn't, then the answer would always be no.

It was during these days of productive grieving that I began to visit friends in the North East. I had lived up there in the late '80s and Marcia, my lifelong friend, introduced me to a local musician called Peesh, describing me as "the punk poet from Essex". I initially felt a fraud, having not gigged for years, and was embarrassed by the title bestowed upon me – but secretly enjoyed it! It got me thinking about why I had stopped and what was stopping me from doing some more. I challenged myself and offered to do a comeback gig at Marcia's album launch in eight months' time. I began writing more and tried out a few low-key gigs… and loved being back. I had previously represented myself under my real name, but from 2010 had been performing a burlesque act as 'Cherry B' and just kept it. (Yes, I dabbled with physical creative expression too!)

I became good friends with Peesh, who encouraged and supported me to perform, and he was the first person I read my old and new material to. After about a year, I asked Peesh to put music to some of my stuff, though he was hesitant to begin with. He played a tune to one of my poems ('Punk Mum' – which you'll find in this collection) and it worked, so we tried a few more, then wrote together. A month later, with about twenty song ideas, but living three hundred miles apart, we formed Cherry & Peesh.

This collection is divided into four sections. Opening up reflects on the early days, poems full of social observation and sometimes short and snappy to ensure an audience's attention. This is followed by samples of the joyous and lyrical collaboration that is Cherry & Peesh. Poems focusing on politics and political figures make up the third section, and it's all rounded off with a selection of intimate and personal pieces enkindled by my profession as a psychotherapist and the intrinsic, emotional value of words. If you want to equate these sections to the psycho-dynamic, cognitive-behavioural, humanistic and eclectic theoretical approaches to psychotherapy, go for it!

Bev Warner AKA Cherry B
May 2021

Don't Make It Easy for Yourself

Get off your arse, get off Facebook,
it's a big world out there and take a look.
Don't just sit there and rot on a shelf,
but remember, don't make it easy for yourself.

Get on a bus, a plane, a train,
make things happen and don't fucking complain.
Break a few rules and challenge your health,
but remember, don't make it easy for yourself.

Try a new attitude, a new career,
drink wine, vodka, beer, don't live in fear.
Don't be in it for the money, forget about wealth,
but remember, don't make it easy for yourself.

Be consistently inconsistent, don't follow the trodden path,
bare all your emotions, cry, scream, laugh.
Don't see life as an invisible secret stealth,
but remember, don't make it easy for yourself.

There is no silver spoon, nothing handed on a plate,
be first in the queue and never be late.
Don't have a lazy reputation, grab life by the balls,
if you make things too easy, everything falls.

So step out of your comfort zone, face up to your fears,
life is passing by, we have limited years.
If you never try, you'll stay forever on the shelf.
But always remember, never make it easy for yourself.

(Cherry & Peesh, 2018)

Early Days

I began writing from a young age as I struggled to share my feelings. I always had cupboards full of scrap paper with unreadable hieroglyphs on them (a term my friend Caroline used to describe my handwriting). I kept diaries, journals, painful accounts of my emotions, baring all with the pen. My favourite subjects at school were English, Art and Drama, where I could be openly creative. I loved drama so much and could play a role and get inside characters. I was quiet and 'shy' in class (I don't like the term 'shy', as it labels a child into personal isolation, which follows through life). When I say it was what I was known as, people often laugh and say "you're not shy"; they miss the interpretation of social interaction. We are not 'shy' when alone, so it only becomes apparent when integrating with certain people – and particular people bring out different sides to me. I have learnt many ways to socialise, all stemming from being an only child. I like to observe and think, watch people and situations, then speak (or write a poem about them).

At age twelve I was told that it would be best for me to attend the remedial English class because my handwriting and spelling were both terrible. This completely knocked my confidence in school and my own abilities to be good at something that I loved. I fought to take my English O-level because they said I would never pass, so I had to persuade my parents to pay for it – and I *did* pass. What I have since discovered is that I have dyspraxia and dyslexia, which has thrown light on my behaviour and learning styles. I only found out six years ago, and when performing I have to have support and help with setting up my equipment. My short-term memory is awful, hence why I always have my words with me too.

In my mid-twenties I tentatively began to share some of my work to friends with whom I shared a house. I found it difficult reading aloud, I was embarrassed and very self-conscious. I began to use the skills I developed from studying drama, of speaking to the audience and walking around. I loved how reading them aloud emphasised the meaning of the poem and grabbed it from the page.

My first ever gig was with another poet. We did a kind of relay set at The Square, my local comedy club in Harlow. I was so nervous, I sounded monotone and the papers were shaking like in a wind tunnel. I also remember that we were given bar stools to sit on stage which just added to my fear, as I struggle to get on them even at the bar! I tried a few more gigs with other poets, just to have someone to share the stage with due to nerves. It always seemed a bit disjointed and mis-matched, so I decided to go solo and began looking for gigs. This also coincided with me going to university and obtaining a BSc in Social Policy Research. Once again, I fought hard to achieve this, without knowing anything about my neurodiverse brain.

Around that time, I also married and had my first child. I played lots of comedy clubs, political rallies and spoken word events, often while pregnant – which added to the set. I also supported John Cooper Clarke many times around the UK, who was so supportive and encouraging. While pregnant, I was sipping a shandy backstage in Colchester and he said to me "drink up kid, you're drinking for two now." He put me in touch with his manager who agreed to put me on the bill with him – John would pay me out of his own fee. His memory for detail always surprised me. Before a gig he would look off his tits, but he was always word perfect and coherent. He remembered every detail shared; he would ask about my daughter and mutual friends and recall conversations that I had long forgotten. I was always surprised at the venues he played in the late '90s and turn of the century. They were often small back-rooms in pubs, with a few old punks heckling him. He worked hard and gigged constantly. Here was a poet with a strong reputation and immense talent and loved so much. He continues to inspire and motivate other poets because he is still unique.

These poems are a selection from those early days, scene setters and social commentary. Picture yourself in the beer-scented back room of a pub, pre-smoking ban, during a decade-and-a-half's worth of Tory dictatorship or the first years' false dawn of 'New' Labour. Words from when I found my poetic voice and felt brave enough to perform, because there was plenty to say. But ask yourself what's actually changed.

Poetical Justice Fees

Your ignorance is blighted by the meaning of the words,
that poetry is read aloud by wankers, twats and nerds.
Perhaps we are sad fuckers who find rhyming words an ease,
but we get paid for annoying you in poetical justice fees.

(1998)
A prompted idea and verbal comeback after overhearing someone looking at the poster of John Cooper Clarke at The Square in Harlow. He was playing there that night and her comment was: "I'm not paying £3 to listen to some twat reading poetry all night." I love that quote. It also keeps me very grounded.

Innocence of Television

Now if Bill and Ben were violent and beat up little weed
or Andy Pandy arrested for making Loopy Loo bleed…
but deprived of Captain Pugwash for having a rude name?
We never knew what they meant so who's the one to blame?
The innocence of television gone from our screens,
too naive to understand what Master Bates means.

(1993)
This was one of my earliest 'performance' poems, written after a conversation about old kids' shows.

Lies Damn Lies

Unemployment has fallen.
The feel-good factor is at its most.
Crime levels are dropping.
The cheque's in the post.

Peace will remain in the Middle East.
There are more jobs in the south.
New Labour stood for Socialism.
I promise I won't cum in your mouth.

(1997)
This was often my opening poem in my early set, because it was a way of grabbing attention – being a poet on the line-up meant I was usually already hindered!

Sunny Delight

Sunny delight is full of shite
and since when did fish have fingers?
They're manufactured processed filth
with an aftertaste that lingers.

(1997)
A response to food manufacturers trying to convince us of healthy options.

Spice Girls

I've got a message for you Spice Girls
cos you think that you're so wild,
but my opinion is that you are positively mild.
You burst on stage with pure attitude,
screeching 'n' screaming, trying to be rude,
but any woman that has ever lived
has done it all before –
yeah, got our tits out in public,
puked on the floor.
You claim that your girl power
will free us all from men,
but excuse me… wasn't it the suffragettes
that did it way back when?
When women weren't empowered
and enslaved by their own gender.
But you just wanna shag young men
and go out on a bender.
So don't talk of politics
when your brain is full of shit.
You think that you are goddesses
cos you're been such a hit.
Your silly games are boring me,
you've nothing new to say.
Cos I'm a woman, not a girl you see,
and my power's here to stay.

(1997)
Written in response to when the Spice Girls met Nelson Mandela and likened his experience of incarceration to their own struggles of being a woman in '90s Britain.

Pregnant Pause

I'm in the club, I'm up the duff,
can't have a beer, can't have a puff.
I can't sleep at night but I can all day,
I whinge about my pains and wish they'd go away.
I can't shut my legs and I can't bend down,
and a line on my tummy has turned dark brown.
My bum's gone saggy and so's other bits,
I'm leaking and creaking and I've always got the shits.
No man could ever understand the way that I feel,
cos they would have invented a nine-month sleeping pill.
Oh, the joys of motherhood, but the best is yet to come.
When a tiny gurgling baby starts calling me mum.

(1997)
I did lots of gigs pregnant and used to enjoy doing this one as it was so relevant. I never performed it again after '98.

The Vegetarian

She's a vegetarian, she doesn't eat meat,
but you'll always see her wearing leather on her feet.
Doesn't eat roast beef, but sometimes has fish,
has turkey at Christmas so she can make a wish.
Doesn't believe in animal testing,
but always buys L'Oréal.
She won't walk past a butcher's shop
cos she doesn't like the smell.
Oh, it's so easy to be meat free
when you do not have a clue,
so cut the crap and fuck right off
cos vegetarianism doesn't suit you.

(1998)
This poem was born of my dismay of certain girls I met who described themselves as vegetarians, because it was 'trendy'. It still makes me angry. I'm sure they are vegans now.

Barbara Cartland

Barbara Cartland lives in a tree,
she announces love eternity.
Romantic novels with fiction so twee,
but with no significance to reality.

Her fickle morals are based on looks,
women are the victims in her books.
The ageing pink princess who falls for this crap
ends up being a spaniel on her husband's lap.

Don't fall for the flowers and seduction of wine,
it's only a trap to keep you in line.
When the knickers are dry and the romance is dead,
you'll have Cartland classics in your head.

Where men are princes and the women in pink,
don't leave wet patches and their farts don't stink.

(1995)
Another attention-grabbing poem. I have since used the same rhythm and style on two other 'Barbara' poems – Castle and Windsor.

MMM

Roll up! Roll up!
For burgers galore!
Every one been spat on,
dropped on the floor.
To have a clown as your symbol
shows what you stand for.
Environmentally friendly?
Never heard of it before.

Another tree demolished,
another fries and shake.
Another cow been eaten,
only thirty seconds to make.
You go too fast to understand
exactly what you do.
Poisoning the people –
have a nice day to you.

(1995)
Written all about a certain hamburger restaurant at the time the longest ever libel case was still going through. I used to dedicate this poem to Helen Steele and David Morris.

Married Men

"My wife doesn't understand me,"
... at least that's what he said,
as his eyes undressed me
to try to get me into bed,

thinking what he says
will change the way I feel,
but married men are all the same –
a side order with their meal.

"We have an open relationship,"
... yeah, but I bet she doesn't know.
Middle-aged men with hard-ons
and no wedding ring on show,

trying to act like a bachelor
when looks have faded away.
Your clichéd chat and manner
might have worked in your day.

Perhaps you might have forgotten
that women have a choice too.
No point in showing off your charms,
should I tell your wife what you do?

(1996)
Once again born out of observation and experience.

Let Us Pray

Oh, you with your righteous way, your blood can possess no sin.
You blame your luck on Jesus and see me as the devil within.

The first stone cast is from your brow as you preach for godliness,
but I, who have no feel for faith, do not abode with loneliness.

The friends I have are mere mortals, while yours can never be seen.
I see religion as an excuse for the imbalance in your gene.

(1995)
I wrote this after watching 'Oranges Are Not the Only Fruit', where religion seemed to overshadow any individual thoughts and became fearful.

Bigots

I'm not the racist one, I've got a friend who is black.
It's just all the others that should be sent back.

I'm not the sexist one, my wife's good and proper.
It's only Page 3 girls that should wear that slutty clobber.

I'm not the misinformed one, I read that in *The Sun*,
so what if I hate queers too, it's just some harmless fun.

I'm not the biased one, my mates agree with me,
I shag a different bird a week, but you won't get AIDS from me.

I'm not the stupid one, my opinions tell you so.
Cos I'm the one that benefits in this British status quo.

(1995)
This was a strong reflection on statements overheard by boastful, ignorant and deeply arrogant men in the '90s.

Not in Our Backyard

No blacks, no Irish, no dogs,
no weird continentals in clogs,
no young, no old, no infirm,
no kids playing in half-term,
no villains, no thugs,
no taking drugs,
no doorbells ringing,
no microwaves pinging,
no lawns uncut,
no doors slammed shut,
no chewing gum,
no dole scum,
no crusties, no clowns,
no disabled no Down's,
no youths drinking,
no free thinking,
no TVs blaring,
no fucking swearing.
The net curtains are twitching hard.
We don't want these people in our backyard.

(1997)
I wrote this in response to a new estate that was built in Harlow. I would hear people say "I'm not from Harlow, I live in Church Langley" and it felt like they were ashamed to be from here. I even heard someone on the radio say they were from Church Langley and when the presenter asked where that was, they said it was near Epping!

Justice Bill

Denied of having a party, now freedom is banned.
When you travel to the country, the police say "Get off my land".

When you drop out from society to travel life free,
MPs are quick to say that the land don't belong to me.

Funny how the times have changed – once we had free speech.
Inflation hitting down on choice is what the Government preach.

Now we can't even protest about what they're trying to do.
Cos they installed a system to curb our point of view.

A Justice Bill for criminals is what it's turned out to be,
when innocent folk are sentenced whilst MPs still walk free.

(1994)
This was written in response to the Government trying to stop people meeting in groups and 'raving' or even protesting. It felt like it was purposely targeted to New Age Travellers, to restrict movement.

True Blue

Who the fuck do you think you are?
Dressed in your blue sweater,
acting like the Sweeney
on a one-man criminal vendetta.

But you never made it to the ranks,
even the specials wouldn't have you.
Your biased racist attitude
even offended the boys in blue.

So you work on the nightshift at Tesco's
to engulf you with some pride.
A security guard with ambition
and a criminal record to hide.

(1996)
Another observational piece, probably influenced by meeting this character.

Cherry & Peesh

We formed Cherry & Peesh in 2017, initially as a weird experiment to mix catchy tunes to poetry in a way that had not really been done before.

Peesh is the singer, songwriter and guitarist of Northumberland-based band, LoGOz. Their songs are well known for having sing-a-long anthems in a poppy-punk style, with heavy lyrics attacking modern challenges. We were attracted to each other for our writing skills and were surprised at how they merged, especially with Peesh's tunes.

We try to make every song different, insofar as arrangements and styles. We mix singing and spoken word; some are like traditional poems and some are like ballads. From our first gigs we were fortunate enough to be accepted to perform at some amazing festivals. It felt like we had some phenomenal opportunities from the off.

We gig and write prolifically. We get ideas from conversations with each other, funny words and viewpoints that are sometimes completely dichotomous, though we have many challenges in our act. For a start, we live three hundred miles apart. We have diverse accents, opinions, beliefs, experiences and attitudes, but we always find something to write about.

We have full electric versions of our songs, showcased on our CD *Electric Potential*, and perform a part-electric set with drummer Iain Murray – our good friend, driver and roadie. We wouldn't have been able to gig without his support and help (and not just because neither of us drive!).

All the music was created by Peesh and some of the guitar chords to our lyrics are included in this section, so you could hum along to the words.

Punk Mum

```
G          C            D                        G
```
It must be very difficult as a millennial to develop your style
Dress to be unique and wild and feeling it's worthwhile
When you're dressed up in your outrageous gear
And greeted with your dreaded fear
Here comes mum what will she say?
"That's a bit tame love, wear it this way"
Cos you try to rebel and you try to shock
But your mum's out partying around the clock
You tell her you don't want a tattoo and she says
"What the fuck is wrong with you?"
She says "Your hair needs some colour and bleach"
These are the life skills that she'll teach
Cos whatever you do you won't shock her
She's a punk mum she's done it all before

```
G          C        D     G
```
She's a punk mum she's done it all before
She's a punk mum she's done it all before
She's a punk mum she's done it all before
She's a punk mum she's done it all before

She's forever swearing but always caring
But then the wildness becomes unbearing
Why can't she settle and just be normal?
Why can't the house be more formal?
How comes she knows every band you like?
How comes she's old but childlike?
Cos whatever festival you want to assert
She's been there got the T-shirt
So how can you rebel and try something new
When your punk mum has done it years before you?

Try doing knitting not gobbing and spitting
Try a country walk not a Mohawk
Try being safe and vanilla and bland
And don't wish to be in a punk rock band
Cos whatever you do you won't shock her
She's a punk mum she's done it all before

G   C   D   G
She's a punk mum she's done it all before
She's a punk mum she's done it all before
She's a punk mum she's done it all before
She's a punk mum she's done it all before

(2017)
Our very first attempt at combining spoken word with a catchy tune and we nearly always perform this first at a gig. I asked Peesh if he could add a tune to this and it worked instantly – we surprised ourselves!

PC World

Intro – D C G D

D   C   G   D
Please correct me if I'm mistaken
D   C   G   D
But has our choice of speech been taken?
Gone too far in one direction
Clever way to use deflection
Curbing our speech – just blame the Left
Whisper begrudgery under your breath
Cos you can't say this and you can't say that
Just hide your bigotry under your hat

We're all living in a PC world
We're all living in a PC world

Has political correctness really gone mad?
Or is it *The Sun* newspaper's featured ad?
But some exclusive phrasing means ignorance is raising
Those who lack knowledge need no excuse
Will spill hate speech on the loose
So what's the answer? Who is correct?
Do we continue to use words that are select?
Cos the reason they were invented is to ensure
We're all fairly represented

We're all living in a PC world
We're all living in a PC world
  G   C   D
(Ohhh ohhh wohh ohohoh
(Ohhh ohhh wohh ohohoh)

D   C   G   D

Yes times have changed but have we understood
D   C   G   D

We used to worship icons from childhood
No more blind eye, no hiding from fear
Cos those that have hatred are quick to smear
So let us embrace this modern PC
Own it don't condone it, let it live free
Us Looney Lefts are only trying to embrace
All the old bigotry that we have to face
So next time you laugh and think we've gone too far
Challenging words like 'black' just remember where you are
Cos the privilege you indulge comes from a bitter fight
Just because you vote that way doesn't mean you're right

We're all living in a PC world
We're all living in a PC world
  G   C   D
(Ohhh ohhh wohh ohohoh
(Ohhh ohhh wohh ohohoh)

(2017)
This song was another of our very early ones, challenging political correctness and how it's often seen as a negative, when in fact it's there to protect.

Bowie, Lennon, Ginger Wildheart
Each poetic song a work of art
Eight-line poem, words that are spoken
I ain't Pam Ayres, twee or a token

Cos rock 'n' roll is the new poetry
It's passion in a rhyme
It's not gentle or forgiving
And fucks the test of time
It's born to be wild and free
And should be for the masses
I'm sick of it being bland and elite
Stuck in public school classes

Rock 'n' roll...

(2017)
The opening spoken lines from this song were originally part of one of my earliest poems regarding the impact that poetry has on younger people – by being too highbrow to be understood. We wrote this version as a nod to how lyricists and rock stars are now viewed as poets and that poetry doesn't have to be boring.

Yesterday's Kids

Intro – **D A G Bm A**

D   A G   Bm   A
Let your music define your taste
D   A G   Bm   A
Don't let creativity go to waste
Dare to wear and don't fucking care
Cos those who object will always stare
So when we were goths, rockers, punks or mods
We'd acknowledge each other with subtle nods
Cos we were the tribes that defined the past
Teenage kicks forever gonna last
It's all about belonging, feeling understood
Being free to challenge if you could

D A G
Take me there…

Never had no money, created style from nowt
Always going somewhere, always going out
Felt part of a community, a colourful tribe
Each individual difficult to describe
Within each world we had our rules
Had our fights and nasty brawls
We would fight for our individuality
To define each section of our personality
It felt important to dress a certain way
But then growing-up got in the way

But you never really change the passion that is deep
Internalise your youth forever to keep
So just be brave, keep your style
As we continue to attend gigs all the while

```
D    A    G    A                              G
```
Take me there, yesterday's kids got something to say
```
A                      D    A    G    D    A
```
Yesterday's kids are me and you...

```
D                                    Bm
```
So do you still have the psychobilly heart?
```
A   D                      Bm   A
```
Or the punk mentality, good at art?
D'ya still buy your suits from a Jewish tailor?
Or new romantic hair dressed as a sailor?
D'ya still wear black? Even to bed?
Don't need to shave to be a skinhead?
Has ya leather jacket seen better days?
Is your tie-dye shirt from an acid haze?
Are your badges older than the coppers on the street?
Do ya Doctor Martens mould to ya feet?
D'ya still go to gigs? Wear the T-shirt?
Does your body overexert?

```
D     A     G      Bm     A
```
Cos we are the tribes that define our youth
```
D     A     G      Bm     A
```
These are our values and our truth
Cos we're still the same but in ageing bodies
Still drinking cider or double voddies

```
D                                    A
```
Cos you can't take our youth away from us
```
D                                    A    D
```
Cos you can't take our youth away from us
Cos you can't take our youth away from us
Cos you can't take our youth away from us
```
D
```
Just give us a pension pass for the bus

```
  D    A    G    A
```
Take me there, yesterday's kids got something to say
```
  G  A                            G
```
Yesterday's kids got something to say
```
  A
```
Yesterday's kids are me and you, me and you…
Me and you   `D A G D A > D`

(2018)
This one was written as a nod to our own youth tribes that were always mixed, as all alternatives ganged together to fight against the dull and tasteless hordes of 'normal'. Also, how now more than ever, we have self-permission to be who we always have been; of going to see bands, dressing how we want and still channelling the inner teenage kicks. We adore performing this one, almost like a rousing anthem at the end of our set as we honour those whose youth cult still remains.

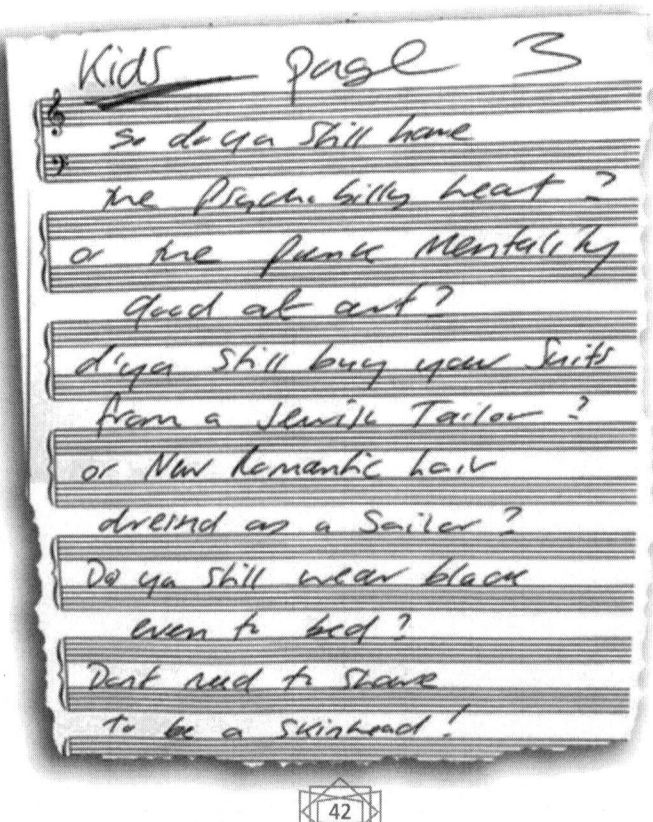

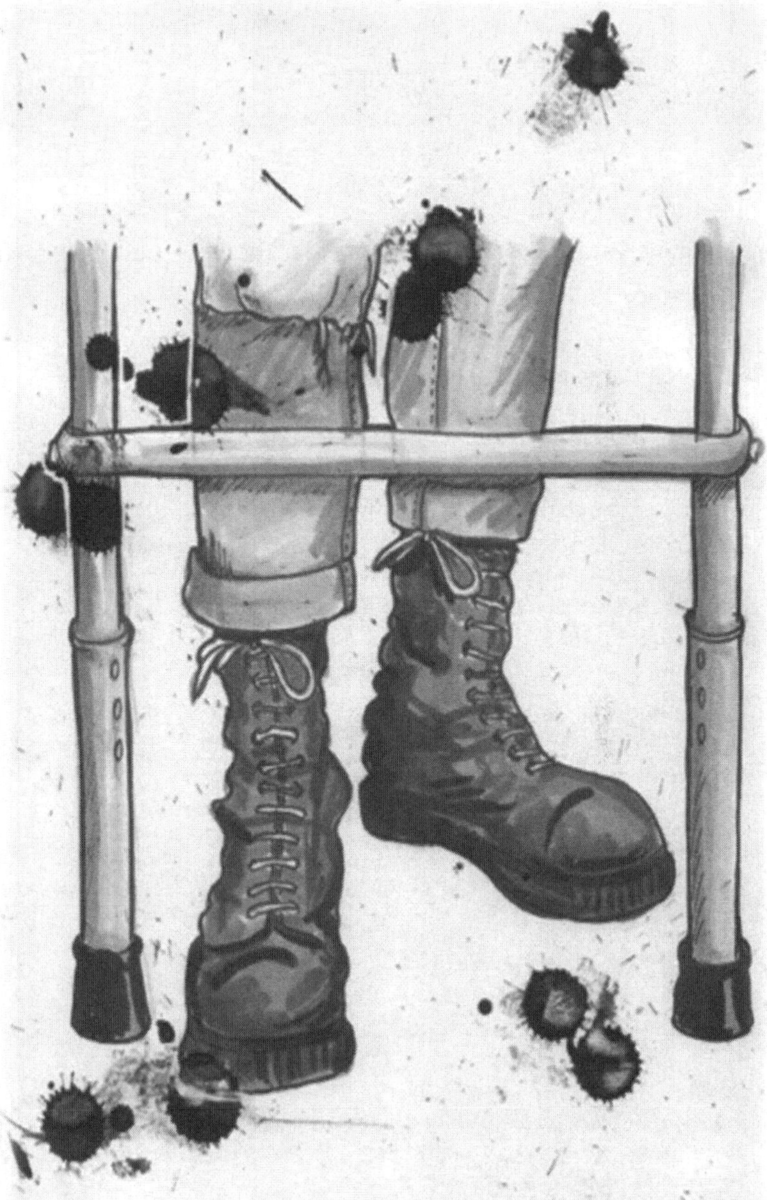

15

Intro – **Am D G C F E E7**

Am   **D**
You wanna be Ab Fab, Eddie and Patsy
           G   **C**
You're the darling bastards of the paparazzi
F
Another TV casualty, we light a candle
E   **E7**
Fallen victim to an online scandal

Transgender issues from father to mother
Can only increase your fee on *Celebrity Big Brother*
The rise of the reality star, creeping, emerging
Till you're all stitched up by your new plastic surgeon

Your life is shallow and pointless and empty
Yet you still have your own fly-on-the-wall documentary
Low self-esteem but your profile is heightened
So you inject some Botox and have your teeth whitened

You are your own brand, you're making a killing
As you act out a meltdown on ITV's *Loose Women*
It's the end of popular culture, that's what I fear
Cos if this is celebrity then get me out of here

A   **D**   **G**   **C**
Come on down you're all famous now
F   **E** **F**   **E**   **E7**
15 minutes gone, 15 minutes, gone, gone

(2018)
This song was about those seeking fame by any means possible, watching Z-list celebrities on TV trying to extend their own fifteen minutes. And, of course, links it to the phrase coined by Andy Warhol.

Ritchie Rehab

Main riff – E Bm C Bm E > E Bm D C Bm

The sun shines through a bus window view
As delayed passengers struggle to get through

A friendly soul in front opens his heart
He's broken not beaten just needs a restart

Faded tattoos and scars on his arms
Years of abuse and clearly self-harms

There's hope in his eyes as he puffs on his tab
Cos tomorrow is the day that Ritchie goes rehab

He's scared of his future, distressed by his past
He tries to stop drinking but it's never gonna last

He remembers his youth, the music he would play
How much he'd love to meet Adam Ant one day

He tells of his troubled life, all that he has lost
The need to drink White Lightning and its devastating cost

He knows he's dying slowly, fodder for the slab
But tomorrow is the day that Ritchie goes rehab

Break – D C Bm A C Bm (x2)

The bus is so busy but others turn their head
No-one else acknowledges what he's doing or what he's said

They don't care about his history they just see an alcoholic
They judge him for trying and this defies the logic

He tells us his pain, shows his many scars
He boasts about his sister and the family memoirs

The sun is shining for someone special today
Cos Ritchie goes to rehab and we hope he's gonna stay

(2018)
This song is a true story of a man we met on a rail replacement bus from Sunderland to Newcastle after a day spent in The Bunker studio. He inspired us so much and in that exact moment we both decided to write a song about him. We often wonder what happened to him.

RICHIE REHAB

Main Riff → E, Bm, C, Bm, E
E, Bm, D, C, E

TAB → E String → 0, 7, 0, 8, 7, 0,
0, 8, 10, 0

Trump Card

Main riff – Bm C A Bm D C

Impose tariffs on goods imported
Alienate nations you once supported
Trade wars are booming in the USA
Play your trump card and save the day

Turn neighbours into the enemy
Build a wall federally
Blame immigrants for crime and corruption
The promised land from your own self-destruction

From North Korea to the Russian state
Playground bully at the school gate
It's the exclusion revolution
This nation has let you loose on

Despised and disliked by Robert De Niro
Excluded from the funeral of a Vietnam hero

A C Bm   D C   Bm
USA won't save the day
A C Bm   D C   Bm
USA won't save the day

The quotes on your Twitter that cause high drama
You reverse policies set by Obama

You played your Trump card and you fucking lost
Now we all pay for this disastrous cost

USA won't save the day
USA won't save the day

You played your Trump card and you fucking lost
You played your Trump card and you fucking lost
You played your Trump card and you fucking lost
Now we all pay for this disastrous cost

(2018)
The song was written and completed but I was blown away by the lyrics of 'B-Movie' by Gil Scott-Heron and wanted to add about 7 minutes'-worth of it at the start. Its message is about the well-trodden pattern in the USA of voting for the familiar face and blends with the up-to-date impact of Trumpism. We still do a dozen or so lines from 'B-Movie' at gigs before the main riff kicks in. The riff for this was originally a piece that Peesh had written for his own band LoGOz. When we started constructing the song the tune was a bit 'sweet' and much slower, but he then played this riff and the words and meaning fitted perfectly.

Society Anxiety

Intro – **Bm F# E Bm F#**

  Bm
Society anxiety, we're all stressed
                              F#
From the crumbling industries and the NHS

      E   **Bm**
Old Teresa believers and your Brexit slump
              F#
And don't get me started on Donald Trump

A united Government, a utopian mirage
Chuck another milkshake on Nigel Farage

Reality suicide, we're all in denial
TV scapegoat Jeremy Kyle

Live in the zeitgeist of darkness reminders
Media mind-heist, nine-leg spiders
Give us what we want tomorrow today

Live in the zeitgeist where leaders aren't wise guys
Claiming to be Christ and damn you with their lies
Give us what we want tomorrow today

Don't read *The Sun* cos bad news lingers
Poisons your mind and stains on your fingers

Switch off your phone, face all your fears
Turn on the TV, 'Bad Morning' with Piers

Society anxiety, we're all full of fear
Misinformed lies from the media

Someone's gonna squeal, nothing's ever real
As we swallow our cornflakes and accept no deal

Bm   **F#**
Society anxiety…

(2019)
Peesh had an idea about the current affairs that were dominating the news and how British TV at breakfast time just seemed to want to scare everyone.

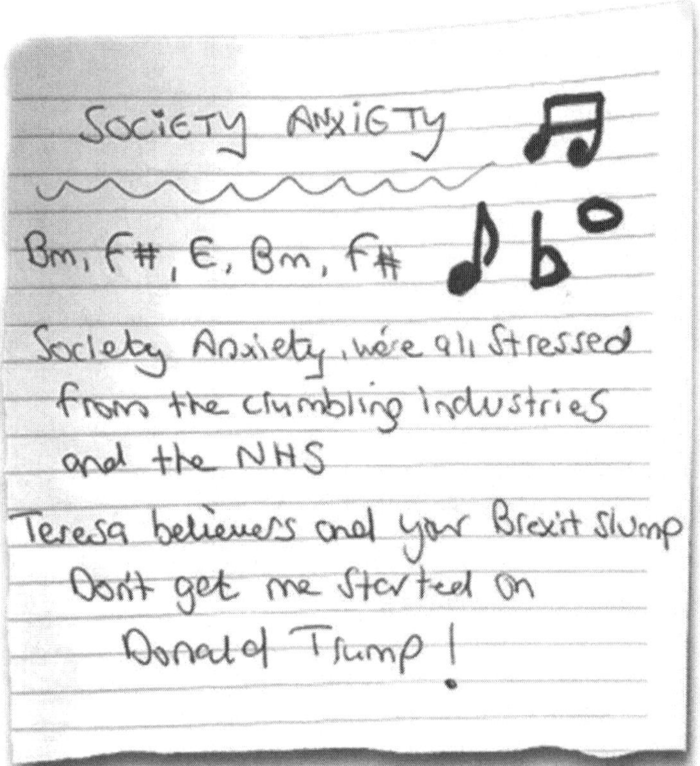

> SOCIETY ANXIETY
>
> Bm, F#, E, Bm, F#
>
> Society Anxiety, we're all stressed from the crumbling industries and the NHS
> Teresa believers and your Brexit slump
> Don't get me started on Donald Trump!

Loan Shark

```
C                                   F
```
You think you're like a gangster from Chicago City
```
         G                              C
```
But you ruin people's lives with no care or pity

Get caught in the jaws like a greedy child catcher
Lure in all sweet but you're the dignity snatcher

You prey on the vulnerable, circle to bite
You harass on the doorstep all day and all night
You bully the defenceless distressed by deprivation
You fuel your income by this lawless occupation

```
  F     C   G
```
Sharks are circling…

Life is a struggle and hard enough
Everybody's finances are very tough
Get caught in the trap of late pay day
And then the spiral of debt crawls your way

Desperate measures not for luxury goods
Creeping sharks in your neighbourhood
Target your troubles with a promise of hope
Then disarm your life until you can't cope

```
C         F            G     C
```
Don't need a loan, a loan, a loan, loan…

Cos you think that you are beyond the law
Sorry mate but not anymore
What you do is criminal
We've got you backed up to the wall

We will fight you with our power
Strength in numbers grows by the hour
We don't ever need to feel alone
And we certainly don't need an illegal loan

Don't need a loan, a loan, a loan, loan...
Don't need a loan, a loan, a loan, loan...

(2018)
This song was commissioned for the Stop Loan Sharks campaign via Keith Newman and his PR company. It is a Government-backed scheme to help eliminate stress from doorstop loan sharks by reporting them and offering safer ways of borrowing money, such as a credit union service. We were asked to write something that could be used as a jingle on the radio and through social media to help spread the word about tackling loans sharks. It probably only took us about twenty minutes to write this and we were so proud of the contribution we made.

Empty Windows

Intro – E Bm C A C Bm

```
E                              Bm        C
We post famous quotes that we haven't even written
  A                     C           Bm
Upload cute videos of a puppy and a kitten
E                              Bm        C
You're looking for love on Go, Match or Tinder
      A                         C      Bm
So you make yourself look better with a Snapchat filter
```

Scroll down your anger, forever it lingers
Venomous vitriol from the tip of your fingers
We impress bitter ex's and old friends from school
With new daily updates and a longing to be cool

```
A              E
```
Where do we go from here?
```
    A          Bm
```
The end of conversation near

You tell of your happiness and your heart is in bloom
But the person you should be telling is in the same room
Sharing your lifestyle clean cut and healthy
We've seen all the evidence on your three-hundredth selfie

Maybe I'm just cynical I know we're all guilty
But I just don't really care what you had for your tea

```
     A    E    A    E
```
Empty windows, force-fed egos
```
  A     E      Bm
```
Digital Apocalypse now

I know everything about you to the name of your pet
But the actual reality is we've never even met
With two-thousand friends my life is complete
But we don't even say hello when we meet on the street

Some see social media as a blessing and a curse
For future generations it can only get worse
Everybody's famous now it's for the world to see
We share our lives in empty windows, a dark reality

Now with extra characters to be twisted and bitter
As I count the retweets on my profile on Twitter

Look at us we're beautiful we pout and pose so glam
Just ask my latest followers on my page on Instagram
But what about the future I'd dare to take a look
Maybe the world will end with the collapse of Facebook

```
   A                E
```
So where do we go from here
```
   A                Bm
```
The end of conversation near

```
A       E       A       E
```
Empty windows force-fed ego
```
A       E       Bm
```
Digital Apocalypse now

(2019)
A song all about the 'Digital Apocalypse', how we are so focused on social media, believing we are blessed with friends, but the harsh reality is we often lose reality.

School Night Syndrome

   E
School night syndrome
Bm
Think you'd better stay home
A
Work in the morning
     Bm
The night is young and calling
   E
School night syndrome
Bm
Think you'd better stay home
Work in the morning
The night is young and calling

At what point did you start to surrender
Have an early night and watch *EastEnders*?
There's a world outside not just the weekend
To go out on a Tuesday you can't comprehend

(Gap) – A E Bm

You'll always remember nights out you share
Staying in leaves your memories bare
Don't regret living the life you choose
No excuse for giving in chances you lose

School night syndrome
Think you'd better stay home
Work in the morning
The night is young and calling
Work in the morning
The night is young and calling

```
E    Bm A      E    Bm
```
Calling out to you, to you
Calling out to you, to you
```
E
```
Stay in your box surrounded by bricks
Bm
Drool over *Love Island* the latest on Netflix

A

Modern technology we all have to thank
       Bm
I'd rather go out than have a Pot Noodle and a …

School night syndrome
Think you'd better stay home
Work in the morning
The night is young and calling
Work in the morning
The night is young and calling

```
E    Bm A      E    Bm
```
Calling out to you, to you
```
E    Bm  A E Bm  E  Bm  E  Bm  E  Bm
```
Calling out to you, to you, to you, to you…

(2019)
We wrote this song after Peesh coined this term, because we put on a great gig on a Thursday night but lots of people said they couldn't go because it was a 'school night'. We persuaded Nigel Clarke from Dodgy to join us for a gig at Ashington football club; it was a fantastic night. Those that want a quiet safe midweek night miss out!

Chemistry

Intro – C Bm G

    C   Bm   G
I recognise the anguish, I see your point of view
I witness the patterns, I was once you
The hazy early hours, the flickered screen of light
Too wired to fall asleep will I make another night?

Smoking dragons before me, I bow to chase my breath
Corpses lay beneath my feet brown ashes forcing death

```
D  C  Bm  C  D
D  C  Bm  E  D
```

    C   Bm   G
The stench of burning foil and the vomit in my throat
Another hour vanishes I'm not conscious or afloat
I'm driven by the fear of the emptiness of morning
When daylight bares the scars and my mind ignores the warning

F   C   G
Don't let me die tonight
F   C   G
Don't let me die tonight

I have nothing I am blind
Sleeping with the enemy to keep my dealer kind
I died in your arms but you kept me awake
Paraded me in fresh air for your own selfish sake
I was craving love what I got was your curse
I got numb for you but it could have been worse

```
D C Bm C D
D C Bm E D
```

| C | Bm | G |

I got the chemistry, I got the bug
I got the chemistry, I got the drug
I got the chemistry, I got the bug
I got the chemistry, I got the drug
I got the chemistry, I got the bug
I got the chemistry, I got the drug
I got the chemistry, I got the bug
I got the chemistry, I got the drug

(2020)
This song is about a true incident that happened many years ago. Quite a challenging one to write but it lays bare a lot of painful memories from that time too.

Politics is Personal

This is a series of poems exploring the recent and current political environment. Of course, there is no hiding which side of the political bridge I live on! I tend to write lots of angry and ranty poems about the frustrations, topical and of the moment, but the respect and love of certain individuals comes easily.

When Jeremy Corbyn visited Harlow in November 2019, I went in the hope of meeting him – but ended up canvassing with him and being on the national news, walking side by side. I gave him a Cherry & Peesh badge (which he pinned on his anorak) and told him I had penned a poem for him...

Corbyn Crush

Well, I was reading *The Guardian* late last night
When a picture of Trump gave me a terrible fright
and I thought to myself, just look at these politicians,
I desire one with more interesting positions.
Then he appeared in a cloud of Socialist ideals,
the man of my dreams on two bicycle wheels.
Yeah I've got the crush, I've got the Corbyn crush,
I've got the crush, cos he's fucking lush.

He's the Labour leader,
MP for Islington North,
but to me he's my missionary fantasy
writhing back and forth.
Let me stroke your corduroy patches,
let me adorn your back with scratches,
let me whisper down your megaphone,
tell me your manifesto and make me moan.
If we were on a train you could sit on my lap,
I'd feed you tofu and you could mind the gap.
Cos your beard is as soft as a Brexit plan,
you're the archetypal Lefty Man.
Cos Diane Abbott, she wasn't for you,
stand back woman, I'm jumping the queue.
Yeah I've got the crush, I've got the Corbyn crush,
I've got the crush, cos he's fucking lush.

Now I need you Jeremy
to stand up like a man.
You didn't fear Theresa,
she was working her retirement plan.

I wanna be your parliamentary playmate,
let's have a televised mass debate.
I know you wanna abolish tuition fees,
but I just want you on your knees.
You're in your prime, you're the minster for me,
my red-blooded man, politically.
Yeah I've got the crush, I've got the Corbyn crush,
I've got the crush, cos he's fucking lush.

(2017)
I still do not know where this poem came from. I had just started performing again and there was an election due – Corbyn was appearing everywhere and had a rock 'n' roll following; he was adored by a wide variety of people (and hated by just as many). I loved performing this live with a Corbyn mask and encouraging someone to come up onto the stage to wear it. Even those dislikers would smile as I acted out the words.

Let the Fascists In (?)

We'll open the door to your smiles and winks,
we'll both agree on why this Government stinks.
You'll make me a promise and reassure my woes.
You'll get me to sign with the party that knows.

What is it that you're trying to say?
That the NHS has had its day?
Our kids are let down at school
under this useless Tory rule?

You are the voice of the common man
who wants an immigration ban,
who believes that Europe is too constrictive
and that voting OUT is not afflictive.

You're charming and subtle
and you think you know what I need,
but I'm not that naive
to know which wolf you feed.

Fascism hides in many guises,
sometimes predictable, but full of surprises.
It finds a way to open your eyes.
Once let in, watch it rise.

So how and where does it begin?
Cos it's not just the stupid who let it in.
Learn how to spot the enemy,
those deluded souls with no empathy.
It starts with silence and apathy,
feelings that you're never free.

Terminus House

No planning permission needed here
on this office block conversion,
14 floors of one-room homes
housed from social conversion.

Half of all new housing
adheres to this design.
It's the human warehouse policy
emerging from a production line.

There's blood on the walls and decay on the floor.
The council house the people they don't wanna see anymore

Brutalism at its worst, the looming tower of shame.
Money making profits from a cheap monopoly game.

It's the urban concrete paradise
for Londoners to try,
but the reality hits and it ain't no Ritz –
they're stuck and hung out to dry.

This is lazy vulturous greed
that the council are backing.
Please abolish permitted development rights,
housing rights are slacking.

They wouldn't choose to live there,
shows their contempt for human pride.
Making the homeless desperate
where the shame is glorified.

This creepy tower that shadows this town
has a reputation full of fright,
but if you treat people like wild animals
don't be surprised when they bite.

(2020)
My home town has developed a reputation for redeveloping 1960s office blocks into homes. They are completely unsuitable for families, often in the midst of factories and industrial estates. Terminus House has stood empty for ages, looming over our town centre. It was then sold to a developer who now offers housing to those most in need. There has been lots of news coverage about this block due to the high rise in crime and it has felt that the council has just let them stew in their own juices, continually stirred by the greed of the developer and financed by local authorities.

TERMINAL HOUSE

Starmer

You're not my first choice,
but you'll do for me
cos you may not be Socialist,
but you'll smash the enemy.

I do have admiration
for the things you have achieved.
You stood for challenging cases
that no one else believed.

You fought for human rights,
both here and abroad.
You represented those in need,
free legal help they never could afford.

I salute you to McLibel,
for Stephen Lawrence, I shake your hand.
The applause from the Caribbean
for the death penalty banned.

The shadow of Mr Corbyn
will always cast long for me,
but if being Left means gaining you
then we shall all have to see.

I won't cancel my Labour membership
until I see your plans
and how you operate and serve
to earn your loyal fans.

You are a fighter,
Labour needs some more force.
You may not be my first choice.
I wish you were Socialist of course.

(2020)
I wrote this on the actual day that he became the Labour leader, where I was filled with mixed emotions. I thought he did have the potential to take the party forward, but I'm not so sure now. So my longed desire for a socialist government drifts further away.

Barbara Castle

Barbara Castle lives in me,
she announces policies based in reality.
Her feminist values are based on facts,
many of her campaigns become Government acts.

She fought for equality, including pay.
She championed women working every day.
She fought sexual discrimination
in a hierarchal male led nation.

She smashed the ceiling made of glass
as she defended the working class.
She joined women as they striked at Ford's,
inviting them to attend the Lords.

She backed us up, not knocked us down,
she was the Baroness of Blackburn Town.
She didn't fall for the bullying peers
and she served for over forty years.

So don't fall for the false feminist like Maggie May,
who'll promise anything to get voted and stay.
She fought for everything to be honest and fair
…but was fucking sacked by Tony Blair.

(2018)
Another poem that matches the same rhythm as 'Barbara Cartland' and was written when I misread an article saying that Cartland was a feminist icon. It was, of course, Castle, so I wrote this to match and make it a double-Babs (though I've since written another about Windsor, too).

The Tale of Yaxley Lennon

Here comes the tale of Yaxley Lennon,
the infamous thug from Luton town.
Thought he could never be stopped,
just contempt of court brought you down.

Neo-Nazi, leader of the clan,
turncoat racist, ignorant man.
Banned from football and the USA,
cos Trump won't let you in to stay.

Front page headline news, nine months now you lose.
Sharing bigot views, tying your own noose.
UKIP pays for your political advice.
Hefty cost for fools' paradise.

Let me list your criminal past,
incite hatred, public disorder.
From fraud to falsity and assault.
illegal entry over the border.
Populist leader like a leech,
as you demand your freedom of speech.
Islamophobia hatred you preach,
don't look back in anger Osborne is what you teach.

Front page headline news, nine months now you lose.
Sharing bigot views, tying your own noose.

We want Tommy out his protestors shout.
We want Tommy out his protestors shout.
We want Tommy out his protestors shout.
We want Tommy out. What the fuck are they talking about?

That was the tale of Yaxley Lennon,
he thought that he knew best.
His sorry figure, alone in prison,
union flag, bulletproof vest.

(2019)
This was written following the arrest and charge of Tommy Robinson, who found himself in prison for nine months. It is actually a song that myself and Peesh perform, almost in a rallying, antagonistic way.

Who Voted Tory?

I'm sick of your fucking Tory face,
you turn up all over the place.
Hiding in bushes at the side of the road,
placards of doom litter your load.
I see nothing but a blue swarm,
I have my principles to keep me warm.
But you? You ignorant fraudulent twat,
line your pocket from the bureaucrat.
Halfon for Harlow, it's a fucking disgrace,
this isn't the politics we should embrace.
We were born from London, working class,
our grandparents would be kicking our arse.
Just who the fuck has voted Tory?
Raise your hand and tell me your story.
I'd like to know how you came to the conclusion
that your superior mindset is an illusion.
Oh yes, you've worked hard, but are you better than me,
you self-appointed bourgeoisie?
Where is your compassion and desire to care?
Lost up the arse of some millionaire?

One day you will need us
when your world comes tumbling down,
but they'll be nothing left for you
in poor Harlow town.

(2017)
There are a lot of clues in this as to why I wrote it! Local politics, merging with national identity, and definitely a vision of what was to come with traditional Labour constituencies turning blue.

Wonderland is Calling

Wonderland is calling and my instincts are falling,
cos fuck all will be the same again.
Yes, wonderland is calling, society is appalling,
but we're far too distracted to complain.

So here we all are in this massive great hole,
we cling to normality, but it's an unachievable goal,
cos everything has changed and my mind has got deranged
and I try so hard to adapt to strange.
I'm drinking every day, Piers Morgan seems okay,
yes, what the fuck is happening to me?
I'm locked down in my feeling and gardening is appealing
and my grey roots are taking over me.

Mr Johnson has disappeared, it's what we all feared,
he has stolen drink from the poison chalice.
We may have sunny days, but it's limited our ways,
we live in wonderland, like Alice.

We are clapping the glory, we are dictated by a Tory
and the mist is coming down hard.
It's hiding the truth from the polling booth
and it's us peasants they will discard.

We discovered new words and much noisier birds,
and have adjusted to things like shielding.
But shopping is a danger and your mother is a stranger
and it's only anxiety they are yielding.

We think we are winners getting free delivered dinners,
but furlough will take away our pride.

We love our lazy days, but who gets the praise
when full time work will be denied?

Don't think that you matter cos their policies they shatter
and the borrowed money you will pay.
Cos front line staff are fodder and they'll all live in squalor,
cos this virus will never go away.

Wonderland is calling and my instincts are falling,
cos fuck all will be the same again.
Yes, wonderland is calling, society is appalling,
but we're far too distracted to complain.

(2020)
This was written during the first national lockdown and turned into a song by Peesh. It captured initial anxieties, fears, frustrations and political distrust in a nervous new world. I actually thought that it would be outdated by the end of the year!

Poetry is Therapy

I have always been drawn to work which challenges and inspires me. The majority of my employment has been as a care worker, supporting people with learning disabilities. I also spent many years as a psychiatric nursing assistant in secure units. As a psychotherapist I have embedded myself in many settings; a detox and rehab unit, community alcohol services, mental health charities, Employment Assistance Programmes and hospices. I have always used poetry and creative writing as part of my work. Sometimes people struggle to connect with their feelings verbally, so poems can give a deeper insight to understanding.

I find writing and reading poetry therapeutic and I encourage my clients to do the same by writing journals or angry letters which are never sent. I have run many creative writing groups within services, with the goal being to allow inner voices, feelings and viewpoints to be heard. Poetry is for everyone, whatever their language, ability or understanding.

Many poems give deep empathic universal insights that enable people to feel supported and understood. One great example is at funerals, where mourners seek the perfect poem about death and loss to share with the congregation. The time when poetry is at its most respected and appreciated. Death unites us and grief defines our loss. I find it such a powerful subject to write about because of my own experiences – and not just the deaths of my dad and son – within the communities I have inhabited, where the thin line between life and death is often crossed, skipped and haunted.

This chapter includes some of my deeper, more emotional and personal poems. They are ones that I wouldn't usually perform, or haven't yet integrated into a set. I still find it hard to share more intimate pieces because of my own vulnerability and the fragility of openly sharing those thoughts to an audience – especially in some of the settings at which I've performed. But I also believe in that aspect of myself being my strength and a gauntlet in which to encourage others to bare their own emotional transparency. It's about how we connect to one another and feel accepted. Once again, poetry stands centre stage in collating that.

Charlie

You never saw the bright new day
that greeted you as you lay.
The sun rose up upon your face,
but you'd left for another place.

The faint fair hair that crowned your head,
I almost forgot that you were dead.
I held you to my breast to feed,
it was such a natural need.

I dressed you up in knitted clothes,
I examined all your tiny toes.
You were the size of a perfect peach,
full-term gestation, you couldn't reach.

You were still born, though you may have died,
you were still born, it can't be denied.

I didn't know why you had died,
there was no logical reason inside.
I blamed myself for many a year,
your distant crying was all I could hear.

I felt that my world had ended,
a sense of life suspended.
Diagnosis gave answers and ease,
I could expel my guilt release.

So, when I think back to that day in December,
it's the positives that I remember.
Although you never saw the rising sun,
I will always have memories, my darling son.

You were still born, though you may have died,
you were still born, it can't be denied.

(1998/2020)
Part of this very painful account of the death of my son, who was stillborn, was found in a letter I had written to him a few days after his birth. The guilt became me and I struggled with complicated grief for many years, resulting in depression and interventions from a psychiatrist. I blamed myself; I was scared and lost value in my own existence. It was six months later that he was diagnosed with Edward's Syndrome, a chromosome disorder that limits life, and that I was not responsible for his death. It completely shaped my outlook on life; that babies can die and how vulnerable we all are.

Be Kinder

Whatever happened to be kind,
a philosophy and a reminder.
We drift away from its value.
Here's the truth, be fucking kinder.

I can't stand bandwagons and following the herd,
or retweeting, word by word.
It's not a popularity show, *hey look at me,*
I'm kind-hearted for all to see.

You can add a frame for your profile pic,
but you'll still cyber bully 'n' bitch.
You want to be viewed in a compassionate light
and suddenly you'll switch.

Kindness is not a temporary post,
it's not a self-directed ego boast.
It's the genuine fragments that you care.
It's the selfless acts that are always there.

So when you look back and see what you've shared,
yet you moan and protest and disparage,
and gang up on those who disagree
and share posts by Nigel Farage.

You seem to forget so quick,
you swap your frame for another fleeting cause.
You share the fuck out of your self-importance,
no room for you to think 'n' pause.

So don't forget what is important,
here is your final reminder.
If you wear it, say it, then mean it,
and just be fucking kinder.

(2020)
Early in 2020, a celebrity took her own life. She had felt bullied and experienced poor mental health. Social media began a campaign of 'Be Kind' and everyone jumped on the bandwagon. But it didn't really affect anyone, people still feel bullied and judged. I wrote this in response, because it's okay to say it, but to mean it takes a lot more effort.

The F Word

Faithful holds no words or light,
it fucks you off when money's tight.
It lures you in to safe surrender
then bites your arse and pulls you under.

Faithful is a flighty word,
never meant, but often heard.
It's a promise made upon a wish.
It's the main meal side order dish.

Faithful tells you who to blame.
It's a noughts and crosses chalk board game.
It's a label given to the few,
rarely worn, the debt is due.

Faithful denotes an honest life,
golden glory to award a wife.
It's the glistening droplet of icicle claw.
It's the Promised Land that don't exist anymore.

It's never wrong and always right.
It's the dripping tap torture night.
Faithful holds its cards and cues.
It's the lost item on the ten o'clock news.

It's the pitiful howl of the sodden fox,
the broken spring, jack out of the box.
Faithful lost its airs and graces.
It's all-inclusive of different races.

It's the battered umbrella on the railway bin.
It's the *fuck off, you ain't coming in!*
It's the lies that layer the filo pastry.
It's the hinted presumption of living chastely.

Faithful has lost its soul.
It's greasy prints on a stripper's pole.
It's a word that should be banished,
like Debbie McGee, *poof* it's vanished.

So when you meet and fall in lust,
before the ready meal is burnt to a crust,
listen out for the alarm bell
cos only Marianne could wear it well.

(2020)
Written with a very powerful rhythm and when spoken it captures aspects of love and desire and deep promises that are both hard to make and keep.

The Family Group

Mother, father, baby me, always ever, just us three.
The cold stone bronze that carved your back
upholds the strength of which we never lack.
The face of Harlow representing this town,
the belief in family not to let us down.

My father came in search of occupation
to sow the seeds for a permanent foundation.
Was lured by the paradise, a guaranteed promise,
for Londoners to flourish.

New-fangled new town, with new ideas of countryside living,
developed with equality and diversity, community giving.
So they came, they conquered, they shared the aspiration,
embracing the culture with true dedication.

They created their own family of three,
Mother, father and me.
It was a poignant vision, cemented forever,
carved oasis of endeavour.

The unspoken symbol of Harlow town
that arose from war-torn devastation
represents the life desired,
formed from planned migration.

So where is the family that defined an era
when the decades have taken their toll?
It's valued and kept as a keepsake,
defines the heart and soul.

Mother, father and adult me,
symbolised forever.
Just us three.

(2020)
'The Family Group' is a sculpture by Henry Moore and is very symbolic of Harlow when it was a New Town. It now stands proudly in the Civic Centre. I wrote this to enter into a competition to do with art pieces. It is a true story about me and my parents and I've always felt attuned to the statue, being an only child. It is also representative of my current family, of me being a lone parent to two daughters, so once again this statue resonates with my life. Oh, and I didn't win the poetry competition.

You Don't Know How I Feel

I'm the shell of a former somebody,
I've evacuated all I know.
I've been painted the wrong colour,
it's only your story that's on show.

I'm misunderstood and labelled
to fit your theory of how I'm viewed.
Keep up the good work of lying,
your fabricated versions are all skewed.

Because you don't know how I feel
and you don't know what is real.

I'm silenced and sedated,
I scream from a hollow soul.
This isn't how I want to be,
I'm losing all control.

The world is turning without me.
I see you carrying on.
But I've no strength to fight you,
everything is going wrong.

Because you don't know how I feel
and you don't know what is real.

My weakness hides in corners,
the darkness gives temporary shade.
Cos you're not gonna find it
and confirm what you've portrayed.

What I feel is anger and the reality is
I'm shedding skin.
Cos what I have is resilience
and your vicious tide ain't coming in.

Because you don't know how I feel
and you don't know what is real.

(2019)
I wrote this during a turbulent period in my life where I felt bullied and this led to my own mental health falling into deep lows. It was difficult to write and Peesh has added music to it, so it might be added to the set. It's important to acknowledge and share these deeper feelings because they are universal and almost everyone feels them – including psychotherapists.

SPAX

I'm a dyspraxic, not a gymnastic.
I'm enthusiastic, often sarcastic.
I was scholastic and fantastic,
but you called me a spastic.

I never mastered certain skills
like riding bikes or climbing hills.
Highway lessons scared the driver.
Swimming, I'm the cement diver.

I struggle with all daily routines,
can't operate machines.
Made to feel like I was thick,
frightened that label would stick.

So for many years I hibernated,
thought that actions were overrated.
Then diagnosis gave me a name
and never would I hide again.

I had talents deeply hidden
where any shame was overridden.
I allowed my creativity to glow
and told myself to have a go.

I'm the dyspraxic, not the gymnastic.
I'm enthusiastic, often sarcastic.
I am scholastic and fantastic,
and you called me a spastic.

(2020)
It was only in the mid-2010s that I was diagnosed with dyspraxia and later, dyslexia. I share this openly because I'm proud to have a neurodiverse brain. It has had a devastating impact on my life; I lacked confidence and self-esteem because I struggled with the simplest of tasks. Not knowing why made me who I am now.

The Valley of Moral Damnation

Lost in the wilderness like we never existed,
invisible feelings have got me all twisted.
External stories bring us regret and rue,
cos no one could believe it was true.
The skill's in the secret of telling no lies,
I'll always be honest, you can see in my eyes.
But the fantasy grew and developed narration,
for we live in the valley of moral damnation.

Nobody noticed and nobody cared,
for only the shadows witnessed and dared.
No footprints remaining, no memories to recall,
for what happened in the moonlight didn't exist at all.
Weaved and embroidered a brand new creation,
one to be admired with no explanation.
It's the kiss goodbye at the railway station,
for we live in the valley of moral damnation.

Who would suspect from the respectable portrayal,
that under the surface is a carriage derail.
That those we admire and hold up in esteem
can deceive and distract us from the fantasy dream.
But who are we fooling with life lived in lies,
when the power of desire has addictive highs.
Blindness can help to avoid confrontation
for we live in the valley of moral damnation.

The spirit of living was always the danger,
yet the flirtation haunting was never a stranger.
Through luminous vision and adverse conditions,
under the surface was immune to suspicions.

The power of emotion made the breeze blow,
the colours of sunrise were never on show.
Yet the ghosts that had danced will stay the duration
and live forever in the valley of moral damnation.

(2020)
This poem is an emotional example of how things can be hidden. As a therapist, I am in a privileged position to witness the shadows of clients; we can never truly know what is going on for others, even those that we presume to know so well.

About the Illustrator

Fe Duncan is a North East (Mackem) artist whose practice focuses on reinterpreting female representation against historically male-dominated portrayals. With work rooted in the history and folklore of the region, its tenet rests upon an alternative proposition of an 'ideal' beauty born from tradition.

A childhood immersed in ghost stories and horror films has further informed her work to celebrate the idea of the 'last woman standing' and explore female identity. She pursues this exploration through performance, printmaking, painting, sculpture and illustration.

Fe is dedicated to bring the political, the beautiful, the macabre and the 'other' together, creating art and stories for both child and adult to feel empathy for the witch, as well as the princess. The results are for the child that she was, when she found that the monsters were the best company in the dark.

A Friend Like Fe

Born in the background of Roker Park,
a quiet flat with floodlights for the dark.
Kicking and screaming as she entered this world,
ready to face what life has hurled.

Schooldays were layered with awkward connections,
with arrogant mainstreams with unhealthy projections.
She made no compromise, no reason to comply,
cos to dismantle your viewpoint is living a lie.

Forced to work at sixteen, her father's altercation –
he didn't want her summer hols to be the wasted generation.
So she worked in a nursing home and developed skills to care,
it made her lifelong empathy apparent and aware.

But her focus was her artwork, college was her calling,
she worked in printing and found her work enthralling.
She later went to uni and got herself a degree,
her fine art qualification gave her work more quality.

But the cause that gets her fighting, her passion and her due,
is the resettlement of animals, from the pet rescue.
Many paws have passed through her doors, kept safe from harm,
but a special ferret called Buster is tattooed forever on her arm.

All the many rats and cats are thankful for her care,
she would never let anyone feel there was no one there.
She supports the underdog, the forgotten few, those disregarded,
she'll fight and picket and help and get their support bombarded.

It was in The Ivy House she worked for many years,
she ran the weekly quiz nights and entertained for beers.
She is someone you never forget, her character is almighty.
You know she'd be in your corner, she's not fickle or flighty.

Yet she still continues to convert, adapt and modify.
She's never frightened of a challenge, she gets scared, that's not a lie.
So now she sings for her favourite band, the mighty Slalom D.
Because everything you deserve to get is justified for our friend Fe.

(2020)
This poem is written about my illustrator in this book; she didn't know about it. I asked her to draw a self-portrait, so once again she has been very humble.

"A glorious romp through social and sexual politics; Cherry B had me chuckling one moment and prickling with injustice the next. I love her positive energy and shrewd observations, a wonderful read."

—*Carol Hodge, musical artist*

"Cherry B is from Harlow, my adopted '80s hometown, and she really does it proud, reflecting life there and hammering home how ridiculous it is that an Essex new town can vote in Tory MPs. Her work is earthy, confrontational, poignant and thought provoking, and her poem about stillbirth had me in bits. She is going from strength to strength."

—*Attila the Stockbroker, poet & musician*

"The art of poetry is not an easy path to follow, but then as Cherry says, "don't make it easy on yourself". She speaks the words many women of all ages feel, covers subjects that delight us by being brought to attention even when they are uncomfortable truths. Sometimes funny, other times deeply poignant and always with a point to make! There is a growing market for poetry and a hunger for the female voice, I believe Cherry B satisfies both. To see her live is an unforgettable experience and to be able to now read and digest her words from this book adds a delicious dessert to the main course!"

—*Jennie Russell-Smith, Rebellion Festivals*

"Poetry is going through a huge prominence and I'm blown away by the talent out there. I'm very impressed with Cherry B and her debut book of rhymes. Also proud to have her and Peesh on our Totally Wired radio station with their spoken word led show *Poetry is the New Rock 'n' Roll*."

—*Eddie Piller, Acid Jazz Records*